Watch Out For The Bad Little Worm

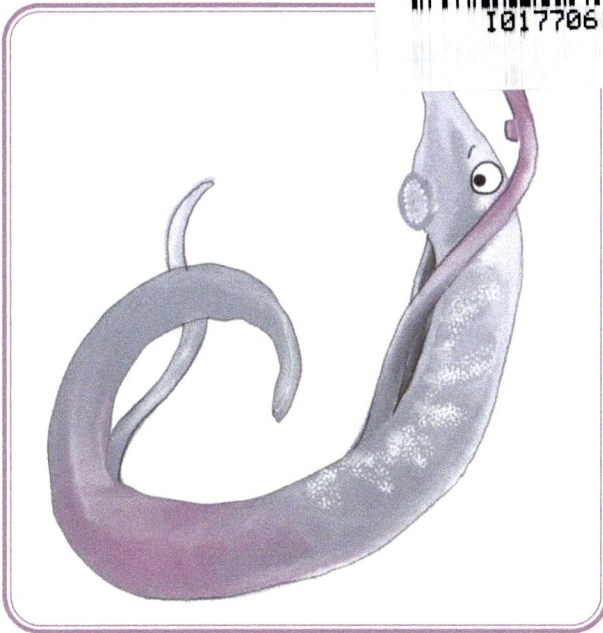

By Savanna Honerkamp-Smith
Illustrated by Marjolein Francois

Library For All Ltd.

Library For All is an Australian not for profit organisation with a mission to make knowledge accessible to all via an innovative digital library solution. Visit us at libraryforall.org

Watch Out For The Bad Little Worm

This edition published 2022

Published by Library For All Ltd
Email: info@libraryforall.org
URL: libraryforall.org

Library For All gratefully acknowledges the contributions of all who made previous editions of this book possible.

Original illustrations by Marjolein Francois

Watch Out For The Bad Little Worm
Honerkamp-Smith, Savanna
ISBN: 978-1-922827-46-3
SKU02663

Watch Out For The Bad Little Worm

This little worm
is very bad.

It makes us sick and
it makes us sad.

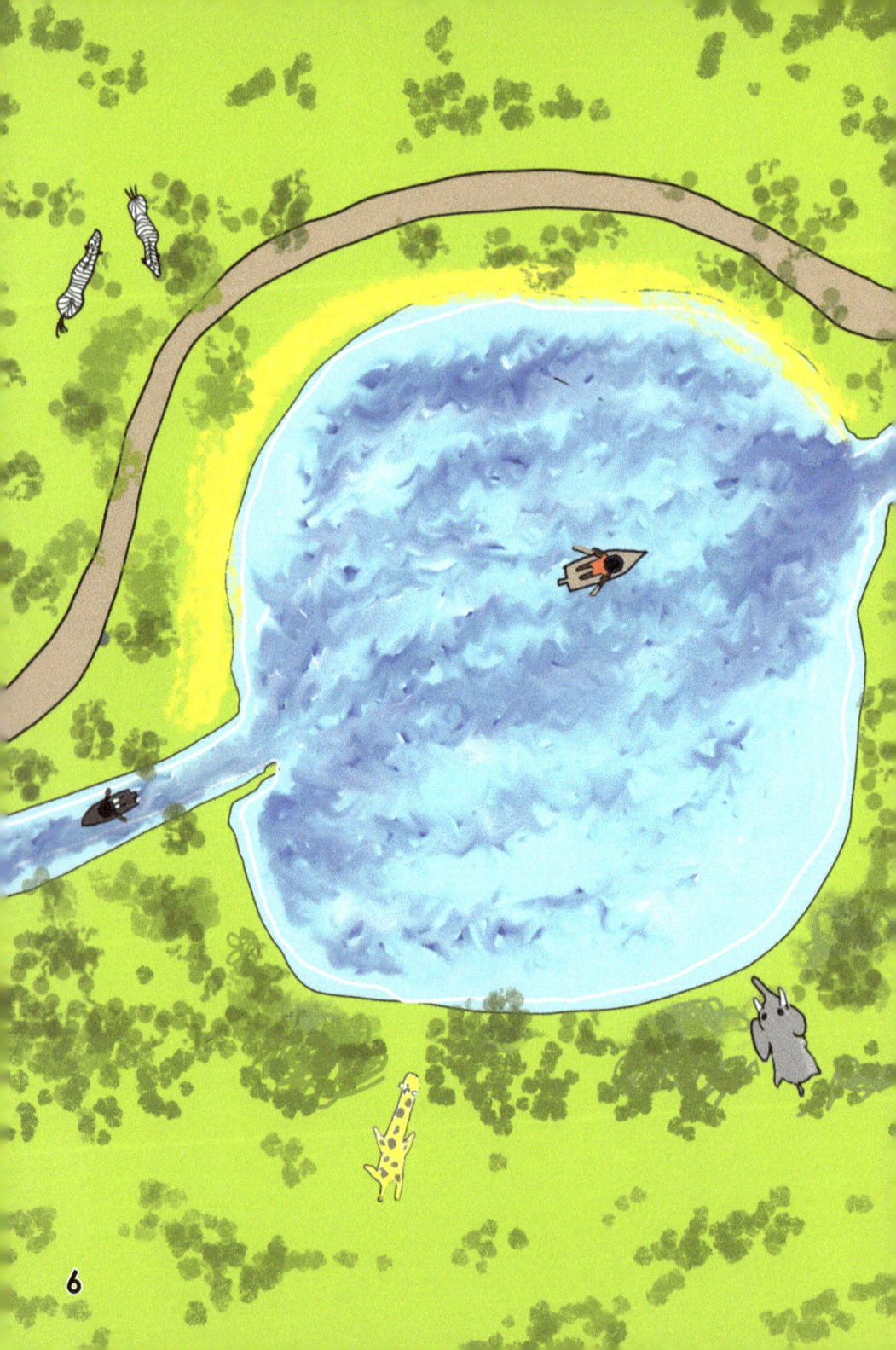

It lives in a river
or in a lake.

It makes you sick
with a stomachache.

When it's small it
lives in a snail.

With an ugly little head
and an ugly little tail.

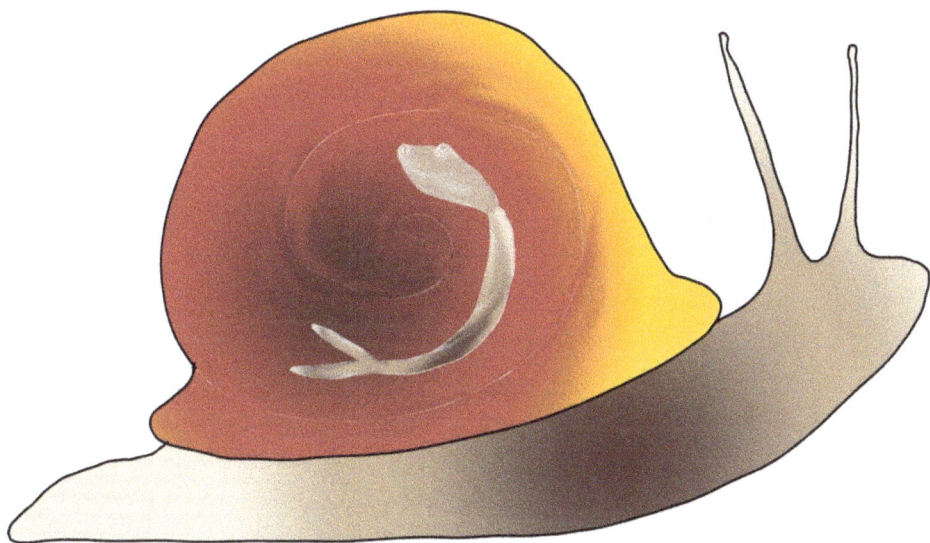

It gets in the water
through pee and poo.

And stays there waiting
for me and you!

Watch out when you wash your clothes.

It might try to bite you on your toes.

When collecting water,
you must take care.

Don't get your
skin wet, be aware!

Only go swimming in
a swimming pool.

And take your pill
every year at school.

Keep your feet dry
and you'll see...

...that worm won't be biting you or me!

You can use these questions to talk about this book with your family, friends and teachers.

What did you learn from this book?

Describe this book in one word. Funny? Scary? Colourful? Interesting?

How did this book make you feel when you finished reading it?

What was your favourite part of this book?

download our reader app
getlibraryforall.org

About the contributors

Library For All works with authors and illustrators from around the world to develop diverse, relevant, high quality stories for young readers. Visit libraryforall.org for the latest news on writers' workshop events, submission guidelines and other creative opportunities.

Did you enjoy this book?

We have hundreds more expertly curated original stories to choose from.

We work in partnership with authors, educators, cultural advisors, governments and NGOs to bring the joy of reading to children everywhere.

Did you know?

We create global impact in these fields by embracing the United Nations Sustainable Development Goals.

libraryforall.org

www.ingramcontent.com/pod-product-compliance
Lightning Source LLC
Chambersburg PA
CBHW040313050426

42452CB00018B/2821